MICHAEL J. HENDERSON

I0467266

The Modern Photographer's Guide to Shooting Waterfalls

Michael J. Henderson

MICHAEL J. HENDERSON

MICHAEL J. HENDERSON

DEDICATION

Dedicated to the memory of Jason Morton, whose life was cut short before he ever learned photography, but whose passion and ambition to learn it has taught me that whatever our passion in life may be, the time to pursue it is not tomorrow, but today, in this very moment.

MICHAEL J. HENDERSON

MICHAEL J. HENDERSON

CONTENTS

MICHAEL J. HENDERSON

MICHAEL J. HENDERSON

ACKNOWLEDGMENTS

I owe a debt of gratitude to Tambra, who persisted in persuading me to start documenting the things I've been teaching others for over ten years now. And thank you to all the students who have entrusted me to help them along on their creative growth path.

MICHAEL J. HENDERSON

INTRODUCTION

Throughout the ages, moving water has been a source of fascination, romance, and inspiration for people since the beginning of human history. From the gentle yet powerful rhythm of an ocean to the thunderous cascade of a large waterfall, artists and aficionados seem to never tire of images of water in motion. Appreciation of the beauty of waterfalls, both big and small, seems to cross all barriers of generation, vocation, and culture. We turn popular waterfall sites into tourist shrines, and wherever there are no waterfalls, we create man-made ones.

The biggest challenge facing the photographer is successfully capturing the raw beauty of the waterfall as we saw it when we were there. But the real trick to making great photos is actually *knowing how to identify a great photo*, and knowing what makes it great. It is often said in the world of photography that to improve your skills, look at lots of great photography; and learning to shoot waterfalls is certainly no exception. It has also been said, particularly with regard to scenic photography, that the best tool you can have is that of familiarity with the subject. Becoming intimately familiar with a scenic canyon, or lake, or mountain gives you the edge in knowing how that scene is going to look in different seasons, different times of the day, under different weather conditions.

Waterfalls add one more challenging dynamic to the mix: moving water. It isn't just the movement of the water that makes waterfall photography more tricky, but the fact that the volume, speed, and overall flow quality of the water has infinite variables that will affect the look and feel of your photos. Knowing how various weather patterns will affect just the water flow is very important. But overall, the biggest challenge to the photographer is getting a shot that has some unique characteristics, whether it be an angle, a composition, or an environmental quirk that no one else has captured. Beyond that, it's all about knowing how to make your camera do the best job it can do to express your own artistic creativity. But once you get that one shot that does exactly what you want, boy, is it fun!

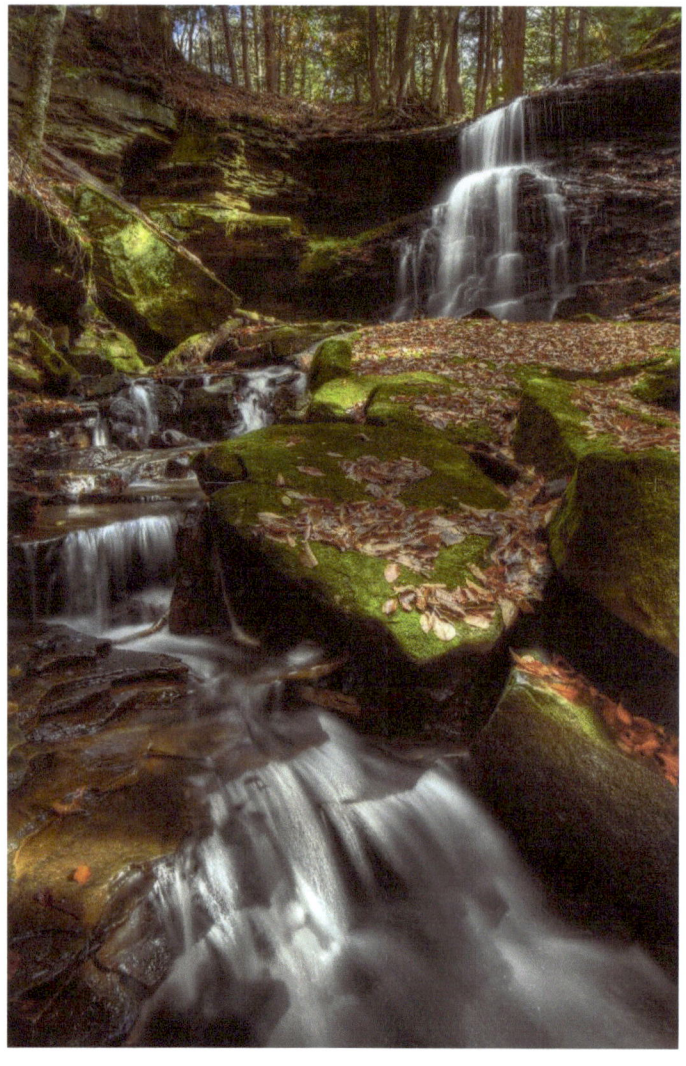

1 THE "NON-PHOTO" GEAR

Before I get into what photo gear is best for waterfall photography, I feel it is important to touch on the *non-photography* gear first. For reasons I'll explain later, the weather conditions that tend to be the most conducive to great waterfall photography are typically the ones that require a little more attention to your attire. Those rainy, dreary days that I enjoy so much can be a bit miserable without a little forethought into how I dress. A good outer shell with a waterproof or water-resistant fabric is a must for days like that. If it's going to be chilly, several layers underneath are a good idea. Just how many layers and what types of fabrics is dependent upon the seasonal temperatures. I've gone out many days wearing just blue jeans for pants, but wet jeans are not fun. I've often found myself (ok, I *usually* find myself) wading through the stream for the classic shots, and water will wick its way up a pair of jeans very quickly. For that reason, I usually wear pants made of some sort of "tech" fabric that dries quickly and breathes well. In winter, I will wear ski/snowboard pants.

I am very particular about my footwear! Waterproof-ness is an absolute, unless it's a beautiful summer day and I don't have a super long hike, in which case I'll wear my favorite Teva sandals. Otherwise, I'll be wearing boots: the higher, the better. In winter, I like as much insulation in my boots as possible, in summer, light and breathable is best. If I know I'm going to be in some extreme winter conditions with lots of ice and treacherous terrain, I wear a pair of mountaineering boots. Their soles have an incredibly "bity" tread that can dig into almost anything if needed, and they work

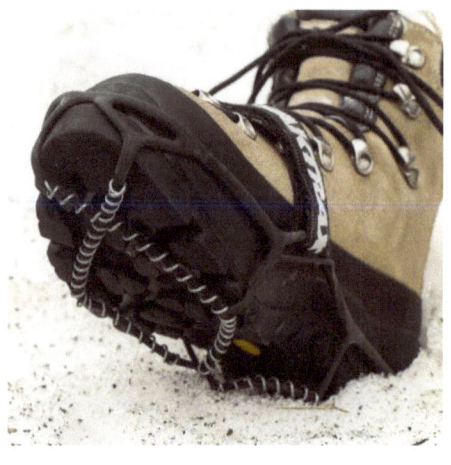

beautifully for attaching crampons or other traction devices. In deep snow, I wear them with snowshoes attached.

In cold weather, a proper hat is highly advisable. In warmer weather, if I expect any chance of rain or if I want a little protection from direct sunlight, I wear a lightweight Gore-Tex™ hat with a brim that can fold up on the sides. It's very comfortable and breathable in the summer, and sheds water beautifully.

To keep the hands warm, shooter's gloves work wonderfully. You can get simple gloves with the fingers and thumbs cut out, and they work great in cool temperatures, but when it gets really cold, I like my gloves that have the mitten pull-overs. When not needed, they attach to the back of the glove with Velcro. The thumbs have small slits in them, so if I need to use my touch screen to send a text message on my phone, I can pop my thumbs out without taking off the gloves. Here's a shot of my gloves doing double-duty for climbing down a rope to a nearby waterfall located in a deep gorge. It's steeper than it looks, trust me!

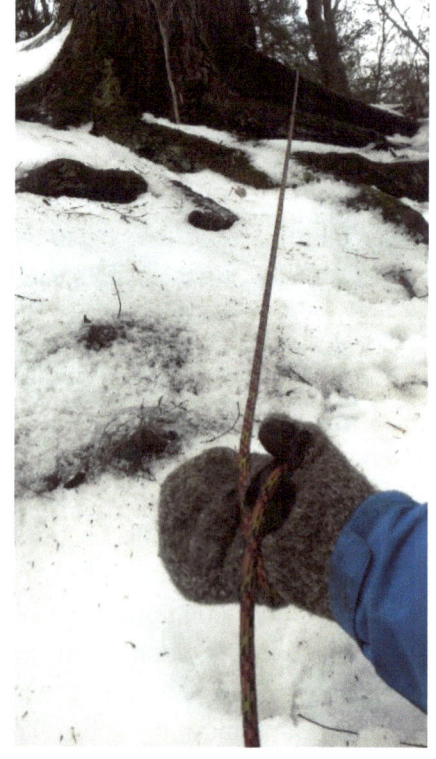

2 THE PHOTO GEAR

Camera

The choice of camera is probably the most-discussed topic with regard to any type of photography, for good reason. But the best advice I can give is, if your camera is holding back your creativity, it's time to trade up. There are many "point & shoot" cameras available today that can do *almost* everything I'll cover in this book. Some are better at doing the things you want, some are not. Most serious photographers will, at some point, want to use an SLR. Today's digital SLR (single lens reflex) cameras are amazing little devices, with an incredible amount of flexibility for every photographer. A budding amateur can get a basic kit that includes an entry-level SLR body and wide angle zoom lens for under $500, and it will be capable of taking amazing waterfall photos. Then as time goes on, the body alone can be upgraded, or the lens, or other lenses added for each specific area of interest of the photographer. Quite often, the lens itself will have more bearing on the quality of a photo than the camera body itself. Whatever your choice in camera, you need to have the ability to shoot in shutter priority, aperture priority, or fully manual. Ideally, you want to be able to save your images in RAW format. You also will want to be able to bracket exposures; autobracketing (AEB) is best, but exposure compensation (EV) will suffice, although it will be more limiting.

Once into the realm of SLR cameras, the basic choices continue. Go with a lightweight & compact plastic body? A compact but robust alloy body? Or go all out and get one of the new full-frame sensor bodies and take advantage of that incredibly rich, high pixel-count image file? No one can answer that question for you. If you plan to make huge prints of your photos and display them in galleries, lobbies, billboards, etc., and you have the budget, then full-frame is the way to go. If you need absolute ruggedness and weather-proof peace of mind and don't mind a smaller sensor, get a "pro-sumer" weather-sealed alloy body. For light weight and a compact package, any one of the less-expensive bodies out there will suit you; just check out the tech specs to see if it has all the features you need. Don't get caught up in megapixels, though; the type of sensor and quality of lens optics are much more important than getting an extra 5 megapixels.

Lenses

Assuming you're shooting an SLR, you'll want to consider your lens choice based on your budget and what you want to do with it. For standard scenics, the normal wide angle zoom will work fine. For something more dramatic, an ultra-wide lens can provide great effects, but the wider you go, the more distortion you're going to get. Straight lines on the sides (trees, etc.) will bow in toward the center. There are times when this is a desirable effect, and times when it is not. Just about any lens made today is going to give you results worthy of making a poster-sized image, but optical quality is definitely proportionate to the price you pay. Pro-quality lenses will typically cost several times (often 10 times) more than entry-level lenses, but another advantage to them is that many of them are weather-and-dust-sealed.

Aside from catching the whole scene of a waterfall, other elements will inevitably pique your interest, and isolating those elements can be a lot of fun. For times like that, you may want to consider a macro lens (for close-up photos) or something like a 50mm or 85mm prime lens, or any number of telephoto options, zoom or no zoom. It all really boils down to how much gear you want to drag along with you.

One lens accessory I cannot stress enough is a hood. Most folks protect their front glass with some sort of optically ineffective filter, such as a skylight or UV filter. I do not. But I rely heavily on my hoods protecting my lenses, plus I get the added benefit of keeping snow and rain off the glass. If I go down (and I have, trust me!) and my camera goes down with me, that hood can be a lifesaver. Well, at least for my lens, maybe not for me…

Tripod

Aside from the camera, a tripod is the most important piece of equipment for a waterfall shooter. Most scenic & landscape photographers already have one, but for certain waterfall effects, you *really* need one. Any tripod is better than no tripod, but I can't tell you how many students I've worked with who pulled out their $15 department store tripod for its first session, only to experience the head popping off for no reason. If you've already invested $1,000 in your digital SLR, it deserves to be on a decent tripod; $100 is not too much to spend, in comparison. Things to look for in a good tripod:

- **Flip-locks or twist-locks** to extend the leg segments. Which one you choose is a personal preference. Twist locks are more sleek because there is no lever protruding. The old twist lever style of locks have almost been phased out, because of their propensity to catch on drawstrings, bag edges, small limbs, etc.

- **Angle adjustment.** It may not seem very useful at first, but tripods that allow the legs to be "splayed" at varying angles are real life-savers when shooting on irregular terrain. The good ones typically have three (or more) positions to choose from, and snap into position with a spring-loaded button or lever.

- **Ice tips.** Some tripods have these already built-in; if not check to see if the manufacturer offers an aftermarket add-on to put ice tips on the tripod's feet. These things are great in the winter, not only to add stability for the camera, but many times I've used my tripod to help me work my way up and down and through some pretty gnarly terrain. Digging the tips into snow, ice, and frozen ground gives me something solid climb around more safely. Most are made to retract up into the rubber feet when not needed.

- **Quick-release plate.** I have always had a bit of a love/hate relationship with quick releases. They add overall weight to your rig, and they are very easy to misplace, rendering your tripod useless. But overall, they are pretty handy when you want to just grab the camera to get a handheld shot, then go back to the tripod again. Make sure your tripod has a fairly universal plate, so that if you do lose it, you don't have to go globetrotting to find someone who carries a replacement.

- **Interchangeable head.** The various options in tripod heads include ball heads, 3-D and pan-tilt heads, joystick heads, etc. Every photographer has their own preference, and the only way you can really know which one is best for you is to try them out. I have every one mentioned except a joystick head, and I find they all have their own advantages. The important thing is that you get a tripod that will let you change the head if you want to.

There is much debate over whether a tripod should have an adjustable center post. Some shooters feel that a center post compromises stability. If you do have one, see if it has a provision at the bottom end for a hook. That hook is intended to have a weight hung from it (such as a sandbag or camera bag) to add stability to the tripod. The center post can also be flipped around so the camera hangs off the low end of it, for close-up and macro photography.

So why is stability important? Probably the number one reason is, much of the time, waterfall photography is shot with very long exposures (more on that later). Any movement whatsoever of the camera, even a slight vibration, and nothing in the photo will be sharp. Even a tripod that is super stable on dry land can vibrate when placed in a stream of moving water, which is something I do quite often. But when considering tripods, there lies a balance between super stability, and light weight. If your tripod is so heavy that you dread lugging it around to waterfalls, then it is of no use to you.

Carbon or aluminum? If money is no object, then carbon is the way to go. But the difference in cost over aluminum can be shocking. The lighter weight of carbon is a real bonus, but it won't necessarily be more stable than a similar aluminum tripod.

A word on bubble levels: You'll notice that on a lot of tripods, particularly the cheaper ones, there is a nice bubble level mounted right on the tripod. Many times I've had folks sidle up next to me comparing tripods, just so they could point out that their $25 tripod has a bubble level and my $200 tripod does not. Here's the deal, unless the bubble level is mounted right on the head, it 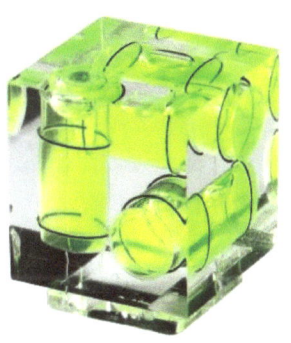 cannot tell you if your camera is level! It can only tell you if your tripod is level. The only way to be sure that your camera is level is to have the bubble level mounted right on it, or next to it on the head. There are some nifty little ones that mount right on the hot shoe, and even a smartphone app you can use by setting your phone on your hotshoe. The spirit level cube pictured to the right is a 3-axis level, so you can use it even when shooting vertically. Some of the newer cameras now have a level built right into them, so you just check your LCD on the back to see how level you are.

Polarizer

Nine times out of ten, when I'm shooting scenics outside, I have a polarizer on. A polarizer will take glare and reflections out of shiny surfaces in ways that no post-production editing can. With all the water flowing around a waterfall scene, even if the sun isn't shining, a polarizer is going to help. But another reason I use a polarizer is to actually cut down the light. My typical style of shooting waterfalls is to blur the motion of the water, but to do that, I have to shoot long exposures. If the scene is too bright, I'm limited to shorter shutter speeds. I'll explain further in the section on technique. Polarizers consist of two pieces of optical glass in a single round frame that's split, so you can rotate one element over the other. Rotating the elements over each other will darken or lighten the filter, which also increases or decreases the amount of polarizing effect.

Neutral Density Filter

When a polarizer isn't enough to cut the light, a neutral density, or ND, filter will do the trick. ND filters come in varying shades of darkness. They are "neutral" because they don't alter the color bias of the scene. ND filters can also be stacked to multiply the darkening effect. ND filters are available either as a round-framed filter that screws onto the front threads of your lens, or rectangular polycarbonate material that fits into a special adapter on the front of your lens. Variable ND filters are super handy, and can go from almost clear to pretty much black. Good ones can be quite expensive; budget-priced ones are also available, but their optical quality is not very good.

Graduated ND filters are also useful. These help to compensate for scenes that have segments much brighter than others, such as a horizon or water line. Using the rectangular style graduated filter in a sliding mount allows the photographer to slide the filter up and down to suit a particular scene. I've found graduated ND filters to be particularly useful at very large waterfalls, such as Niagara Falls, on bright sunny days.

Remote Shutter Release

Whether via cable or wireless, a remote shutter device comes in handy, particularly if you need to time your exposures precisely. I've found, however, that I've gotten just a tad lazy over the years, and instead of bothering to pull mine out of my bag and plug it in, I just use the 2-second timer. It gives me just enough time to back away and let the camera fire without being bumped or jostled.

Umbrella

If you find yourself prone to shooting in rain, drizzle, fog, snow, or other damp weather, an umbrella isn't a bad idea. Not necessarily for yourself, but for your camera. You can also get brackets to attach umbrellas to a tripod, so you have both hands free. This is especially important if you want to shoot in inclement weather and your camera body isn't weather-sealed. A translucent white umbrella can also double as a light diffuser or reflector for small scenes such as with a macro lens. A black umbrella can serve as a dark background in macro shots.

3 COMPOSITION

Perhaps the most subjective part of photography, composition can often be strictly personal taste. There are rules, but as the saying goes, rules are meant to be broken. However, it is difficult to know you're breaking the rules if you don't know what they are in the first place. With that in mind, the rule of thirds is a great place to start. Imagine your scene divided up into 9 squares, or rectangles, 3 across, and 3 down. Putting key elements of your scene into the upper, lower, left, and right third area makes the image more aesthetically pleasing to the eye. If you don't believe this, take a look at photos you really like, place an imaginary grid over them, and see what happens. If you use Photoshop, you can create your own Rule of Thirds grid by navigating to Preferences → Guides, Grid & Slices and change Gridline every 100 percent, Subdivisions 3. Toggle your grid off and on by using CTRL-' (apostrophe), or Command-' on a Mac.

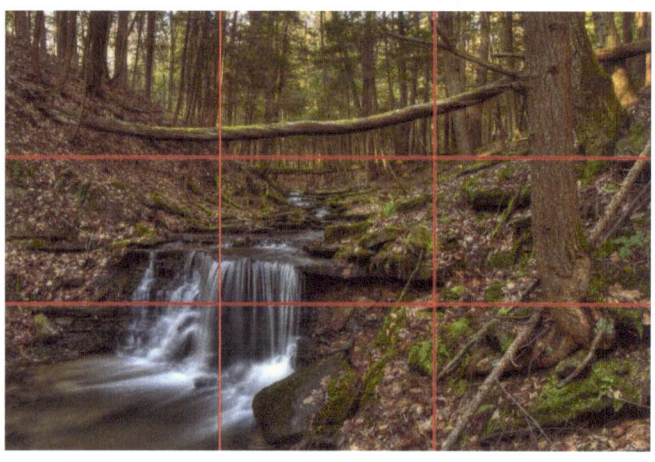

Another thing to look for in your scene is framing. Use trees,

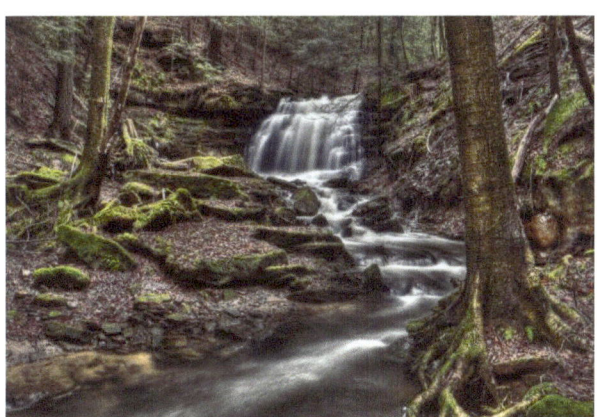

branches, rock formations to frame your scene around the edges. Quite often I look for interesting trees that may contribute to the look and feel of the textures, as well as frame the main subject.

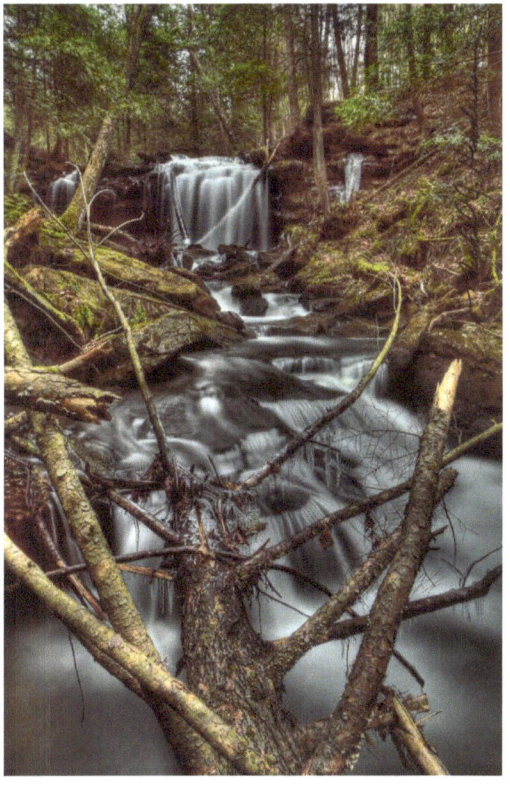

These elements can also be used as leading lines, which lead the viewer's eyes toward the main subject, which in this case, is often the waterfall itself. Sometimes a composition will find you, rather than the other way around, if you stay open-minded. Here's a waterfall where I desperately wanted to find a different angle, something I hadn't done before. But all this debris kept getting in the way, including this newly-fallen hemlock. Suddenly I realized I could make the waterfall secondary and the fallen tree primary elements in my photo. When I got home and reviewed my photos, I was very pleasantly surprised.

Every time I shoot this waterfall, the old stump just jumps out at me. It has become the signature element of this one for me.

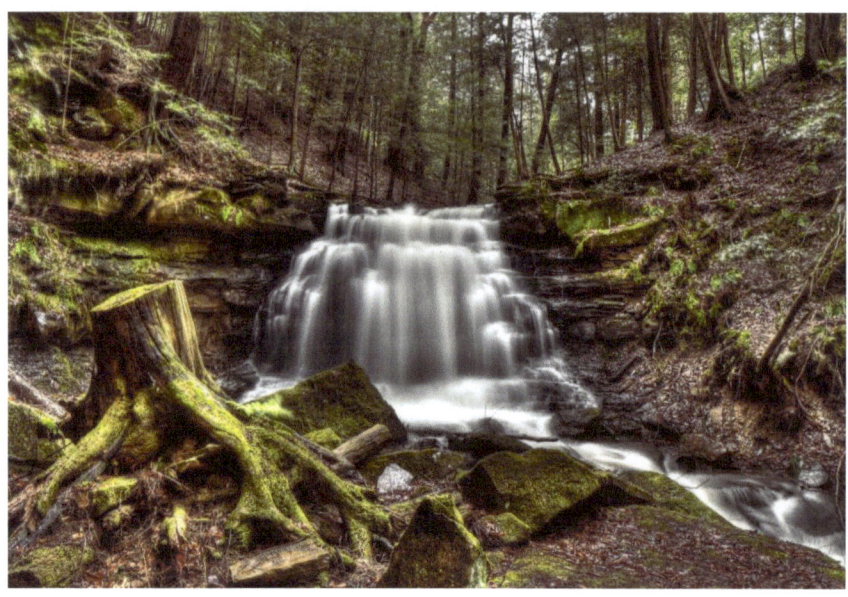

Horizontal or vertical? Horizontally-oriented photos are traditionally referred to as "landscape," therefore, it seems natural to shoot a landscape horizontally. But waterfalls tend to tempt us more to shoot vertically (or traditionally, "portrait") than other types of scenic subjects. It is beneficial to maintain an open mind and try many different angles and orientations. Take your time and view the scene as many different ways as you can; you may be pleasantly surprised to find something totally different than you were expecting.

"Get close. Get closer."

One of my very gifted nature photographer friends, John Karian, says this all the time. Sometimes when I'm out there looking for inspiration, those words come back to me. While shooting the previous photo, I started looking for interesting scenes within the scene, and I started spotting unique little ice formations just above the water; so I got closer and captured their beauty.

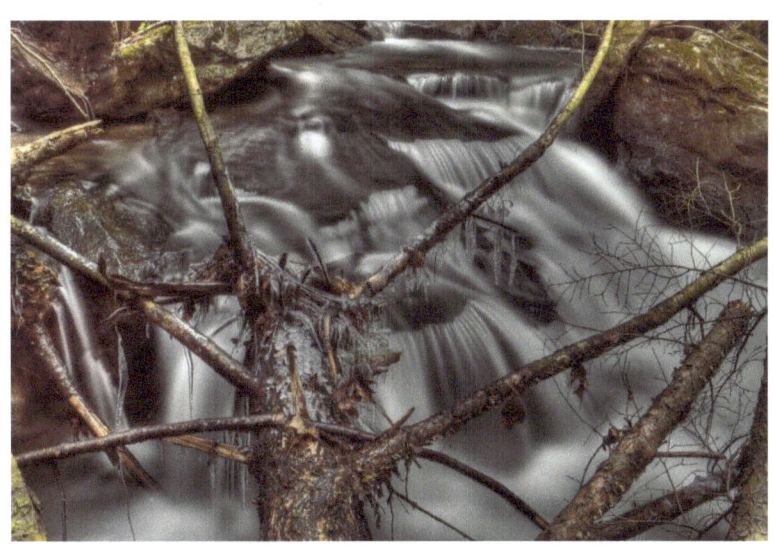

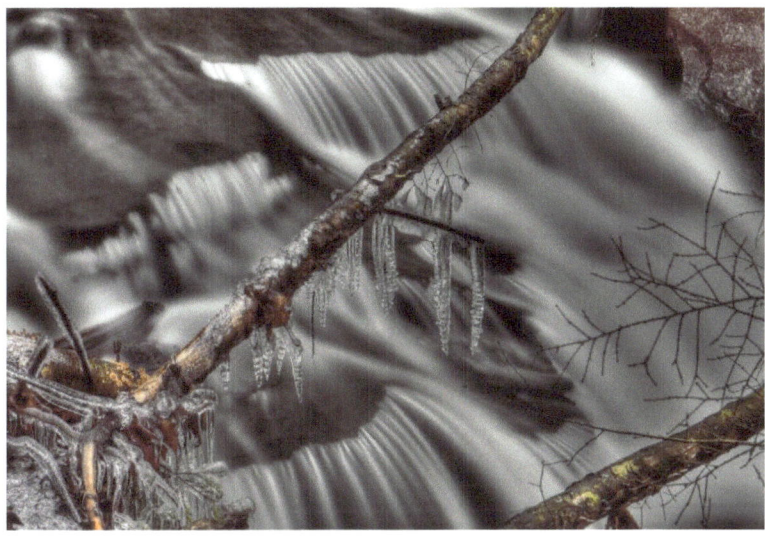

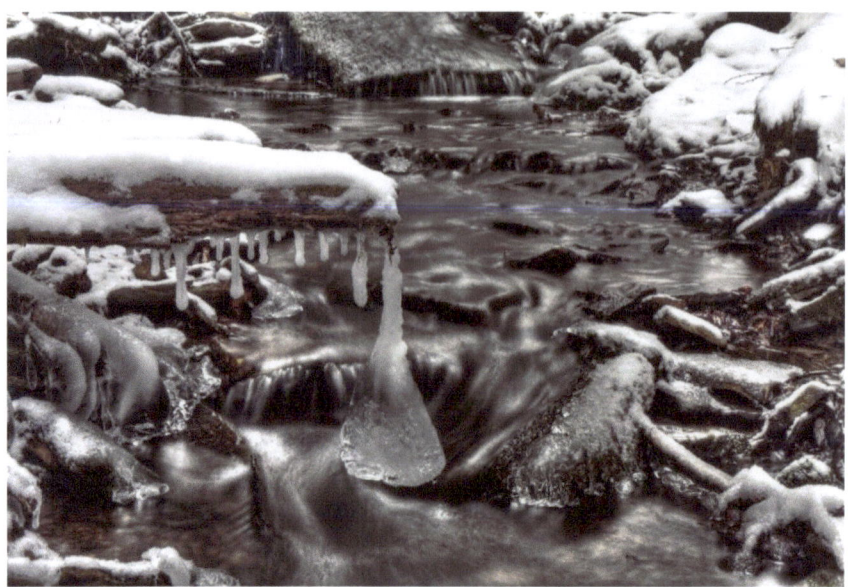

Don't forget the non-waterfall subjects, either! Sometimes just turning around and looking behind you yields some great subject material.

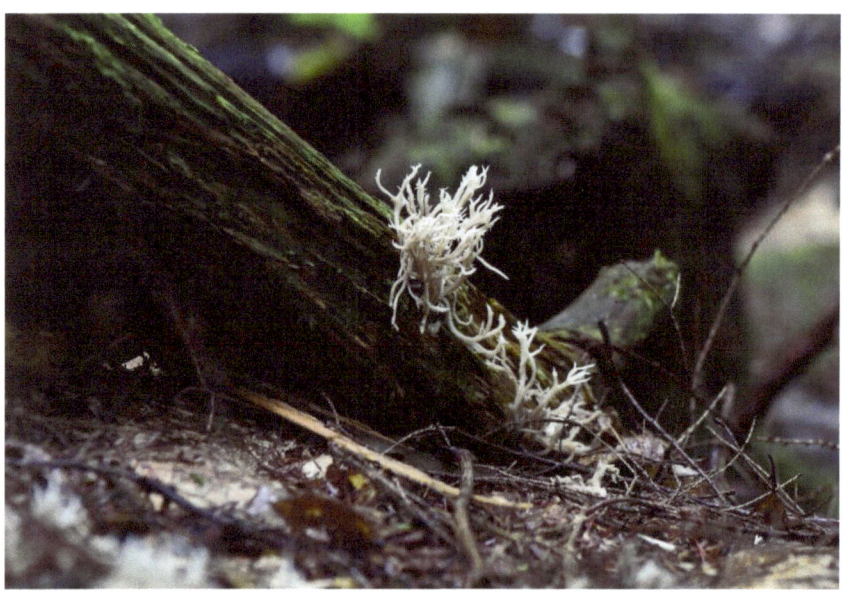

It is truly a magical time in the forest when the trilliums are in bloom.

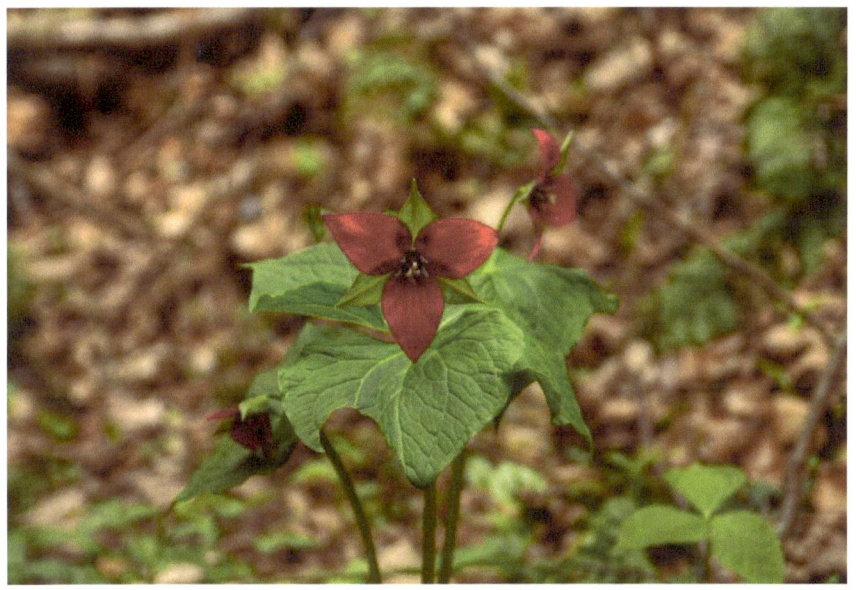

Last year I was visiting one of my regular local waterfalls, and I discovered that even during low water level periods, interesting things can happen. I was working along the actual face of the waterfall when I stumbled onto this fascinating feature. See the weeping Indian?

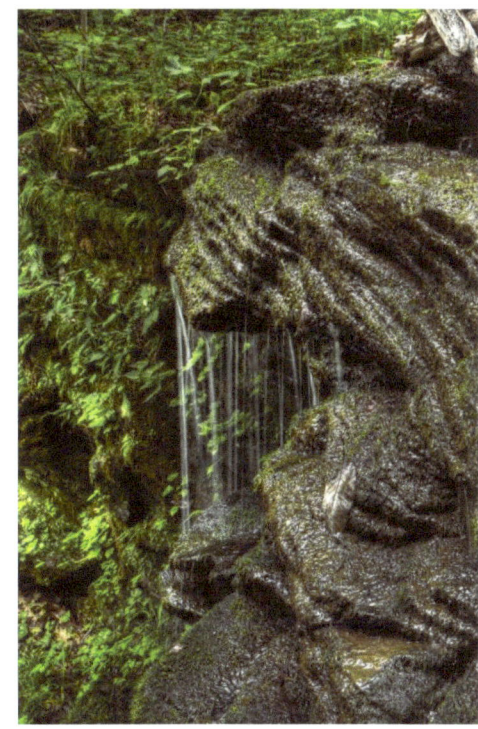

A couple years ago I had some free time to go out shooting and the conditions were just the way I like them, dreary with a bit of fog, after some extended rain. So I set out for the old standby in my area, Freedom Falls. But try as I might, I just could not get inspired. I used up half a memory card, then I decided to give up and head home. Here's the road leading up the hill from the falls.

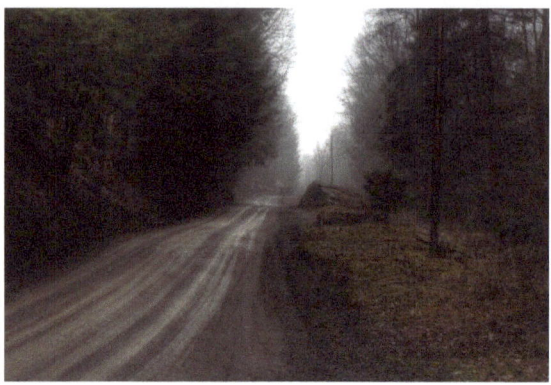

It was getting dark, so I figured I was done for the day. But as I approached the top of the hill, I glanced down into the ravine and saw a section I'd never noticed before. I parked and walked down to the creek as the evening darkness began to creep in. I was really liking this section that had escaped me on dozens of trips I'd made to Freedom Falls. Here's one of the shots I got after it had gotten so dark that I needed a flashlight to see the controls on my camera!

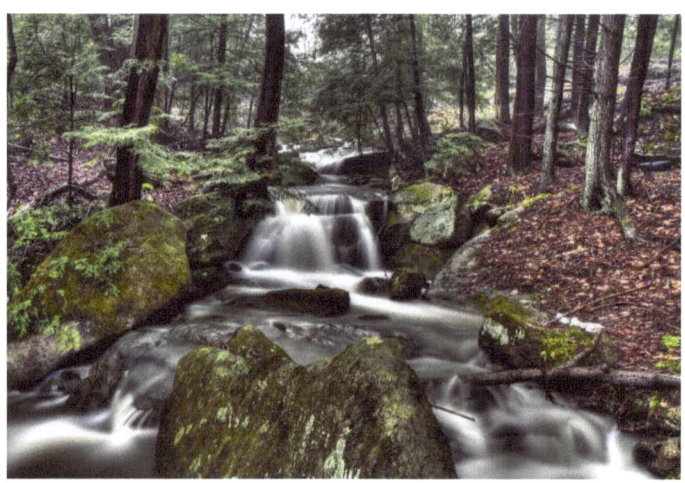

Here is a vertical composition from the same spot, using a wild grape vine as a framing element. I could barely make out the outline of the vine, so I was pretty happy when I got home to discover that I had gotten it in the frame.

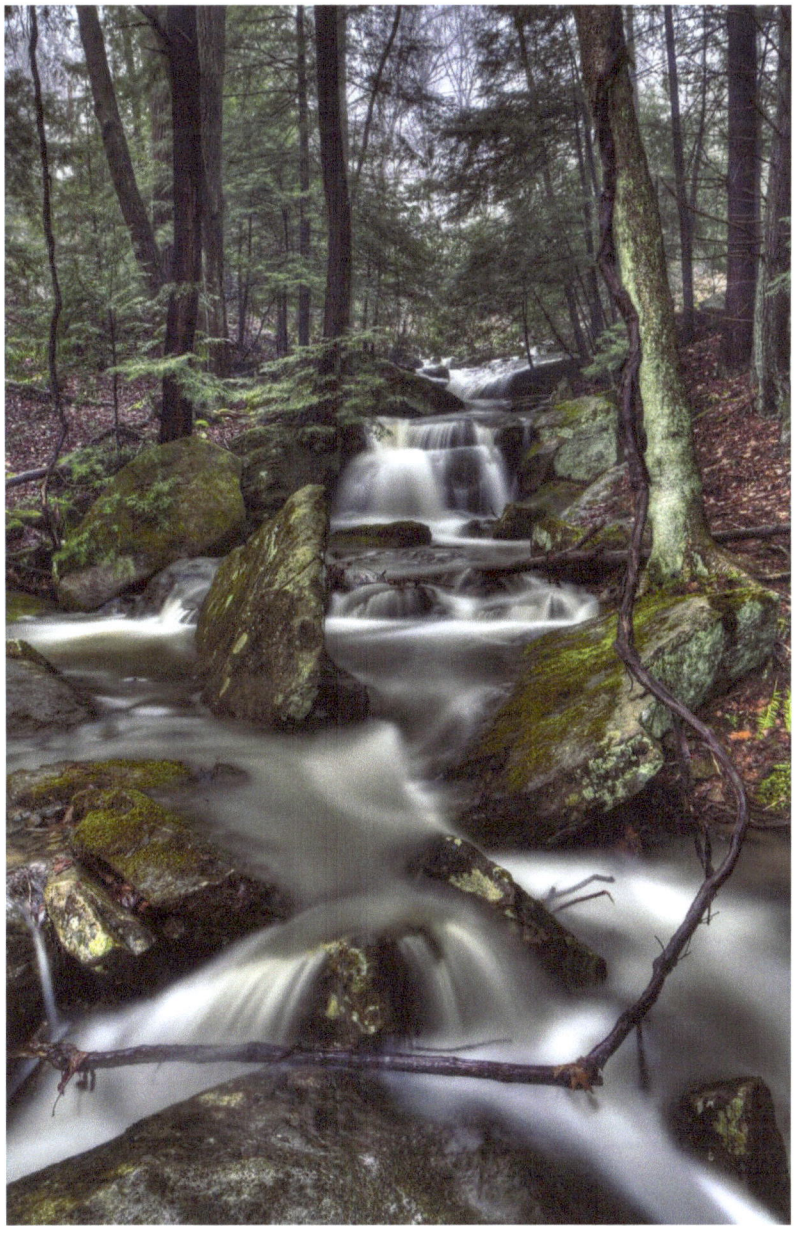

4 WEATHER

For my taste, the absolute best weather for shooting waterfalls is the weather that keeps most folks indoors by a comfy fire. Dreary, overcast days provide the best light for moody scenic photography. Low contrast gives the camera the ability to capture more detail at each end of the light scale (dynamic range, luminosity, etc.) Colors become more saturated when the sun's light is diffused through clouds, fog, etc. But if your camera isn't built to handle a lot of moisture, you'll need to take precautions. As mentioned above in the gear section, an umbrella comes in handy to keep your camera dry while shooting on a tripod. My camera body has weather sealing, so it can take quite a bit of abuse before permanent damage sets in. Here's an example of what it looks like on a typical snowy day. Good thing I had the lens hood on!

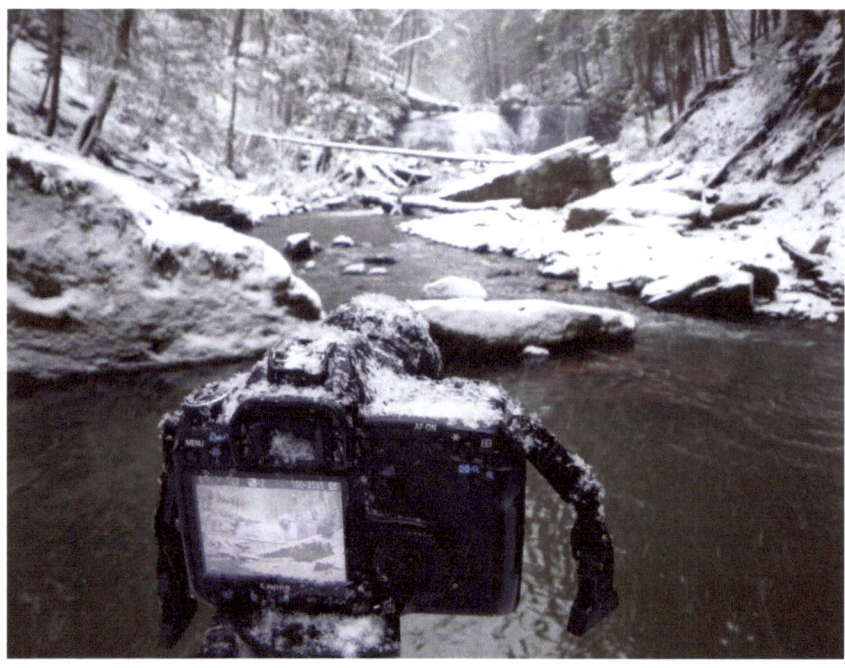

Here's a shot of one of my local waterfalls on a very dreary, drizzly day. See how it sets a mood?

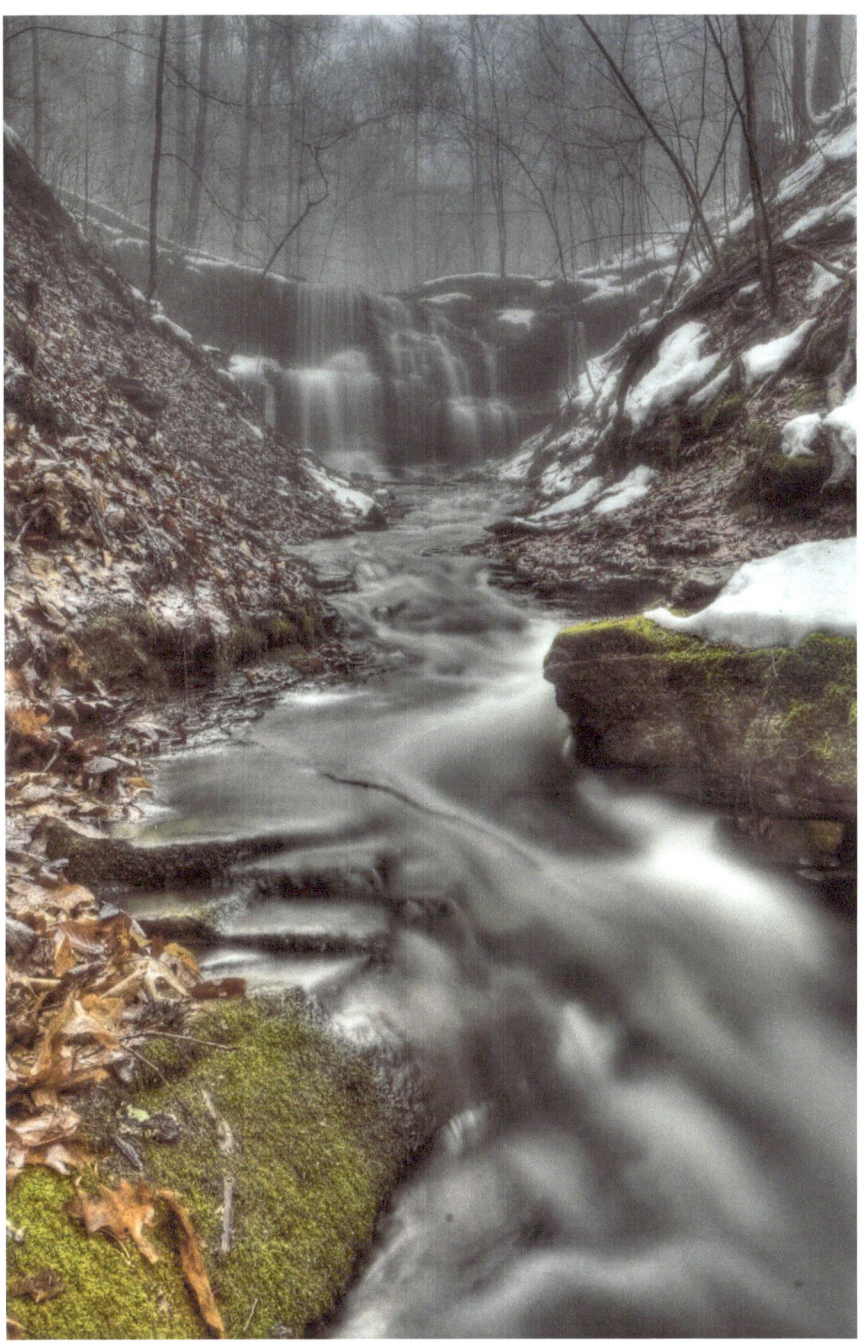

Of course, wintertime can create its own set of challenges aside from getting your camera wet. Here's my Jeep in snow up to its hubs during one of my winter outings.

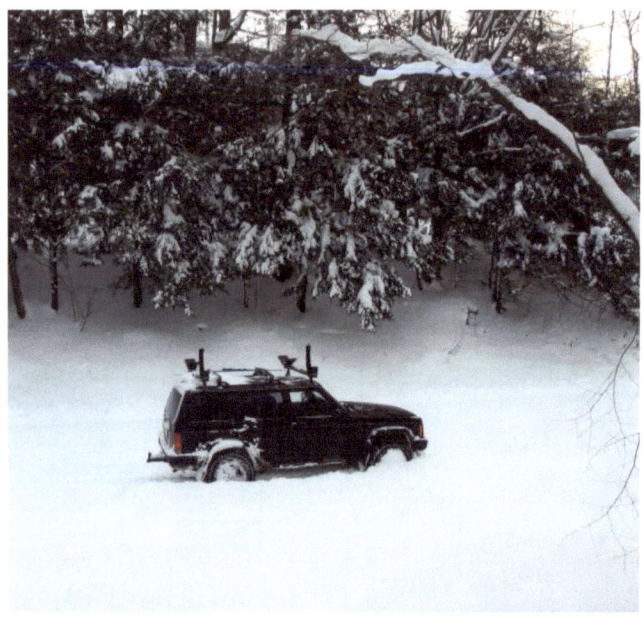

But the payoff always makes it worthwhile.

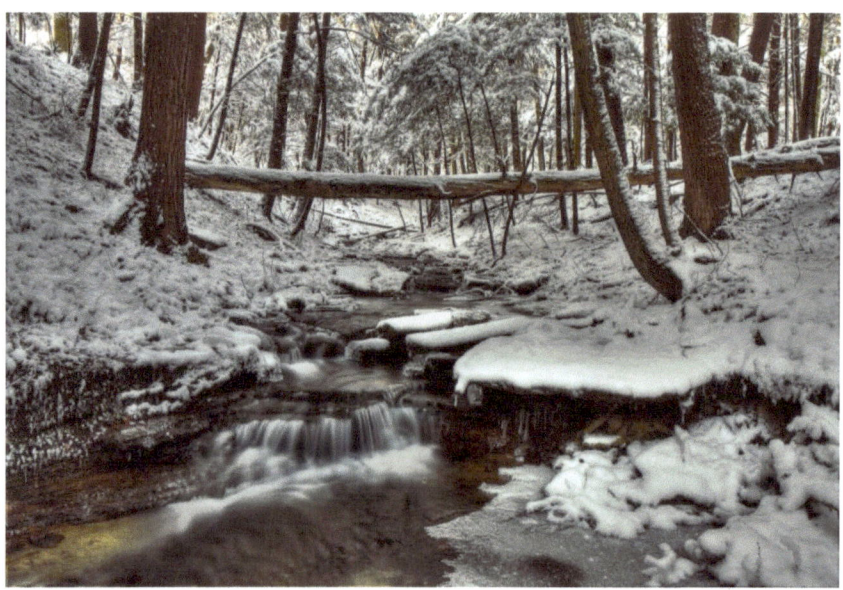

During snowmelt and occasional flash floods, the streamflow can be quite spectacular. There are some folks who feel that muddy-colored water is not desirable; but sometimes the contrast can be interesting.

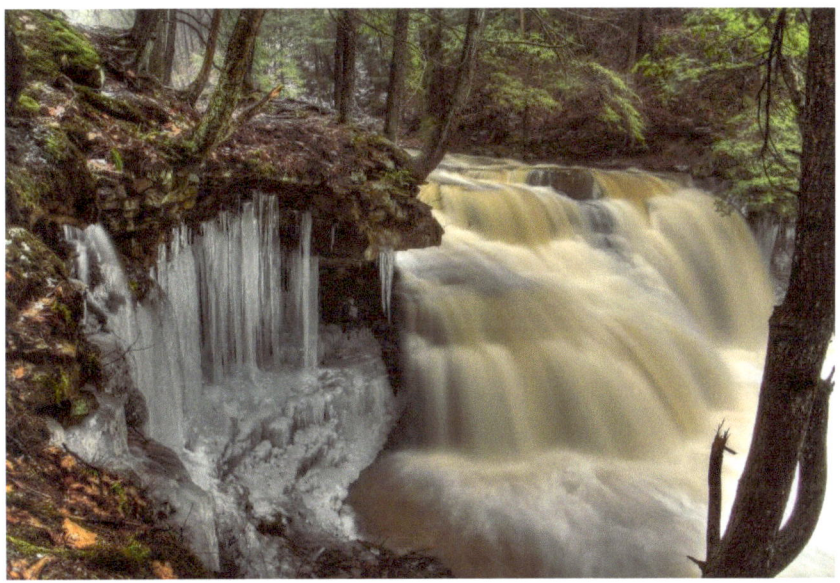

Here is the same waterfall from a different angle.

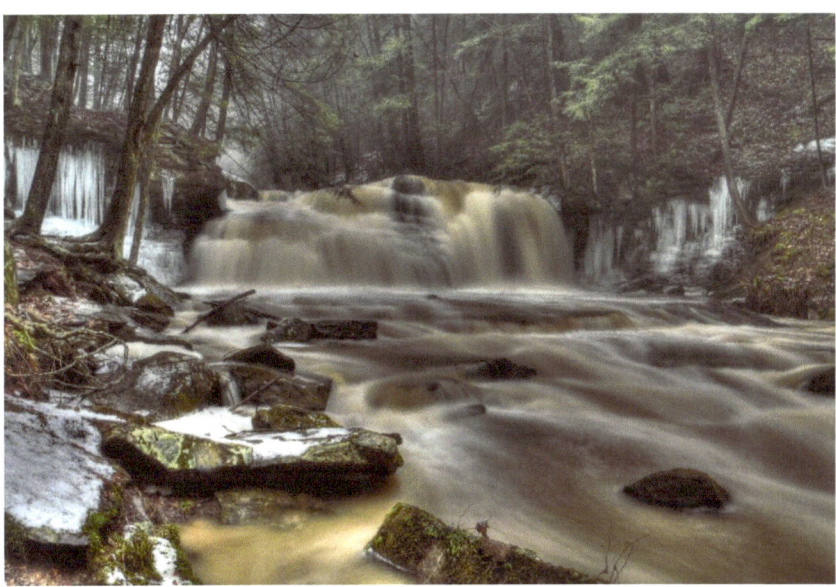

5 TECHNIQUE

Disclaimer: There is an assumption made on my part that you understand the basics of how to set proper exposures with your camera, and that you are comfortable with shooting in modes other than full auto. It would be a waste of space and time to go into all of that here, especially since every camera brand and model is different, so instruction on the various modes for all those cameras would go way beyond the scope of this book. If you have not yet gotten comfortable with shooting in manual and semi-manual modes, I highly recommend getting into your manufacturer's manual or checking out any of the very helpful aftermarket tutorials and books available on the subject that are specific to your particular make and model of camera.

Motion Blur

Probably the number one thing about waterfall photography that creates something of a divide is the blurred water effect. While the majority of viewers appreciate and enjoy the effect, there is still a minority who do not. Like composition, this is definitely a matter of personal taste, and also depends on what the photographer wants to convey. If individual water droplets caught mid-air is the desired effect, you certainly would not want to induce blur, so a faster shutter speed would be necessary.

To achieve motion blur of the moving water, you need to slow the shutter down, a lot. For a beginning photographer, this tends to go against natural instinct; but remember, here is where the tripod is your friend. With your camera perched atop a stable tripod, the only thing that will be blurred with a long exposure is whatever in the scene is moving. Keep in mind, this means not only moving water, but windblown trees, leaves, ferns, etc. So, if you plan to use this effect, make sure you're aware of what's moving and what the wind is doing. I've found that I can get away with a little bit of movement in the scene, but too much and things start getting too distracting. Of course, if you wanted to experiment with different windblown effects, there's always room to play with it. After all, it's digital! Anything you don't like, you can delete.

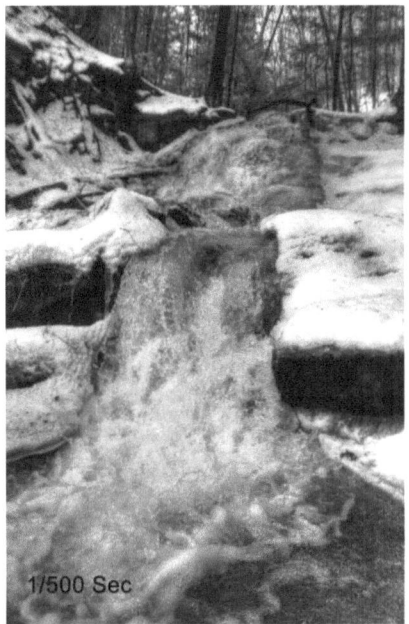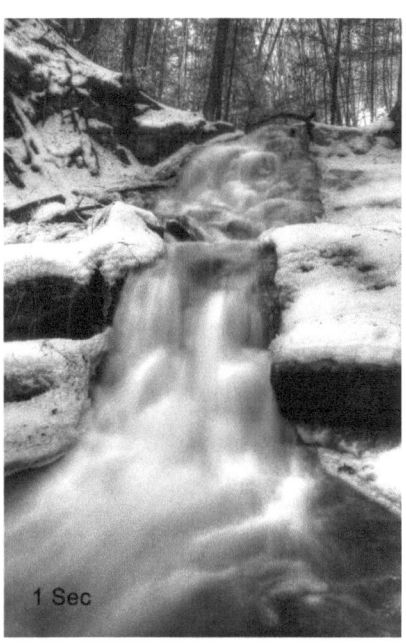

So, how to slow down the shutter, and how much? Let me answer the second part first. How much you leave the shutter open is dependent upon the speed of the flowing water and the amount of blur you desire. While I've gone as far as 30 seconds on an exposure, you probably won't see much difference after 5. The most noticeable differences will likely be between 1/125 and 1 second. To catch the water droplets in razor-sharp detail, I'd recommend 1/125 or higher. In fact, by using flash, you can capture motion as quickly as 1/10,000 second or faster.

Here's a progressive series showing increments equal to one f-stop between each frame, from 1/1,000 second to 2.5 seconds.

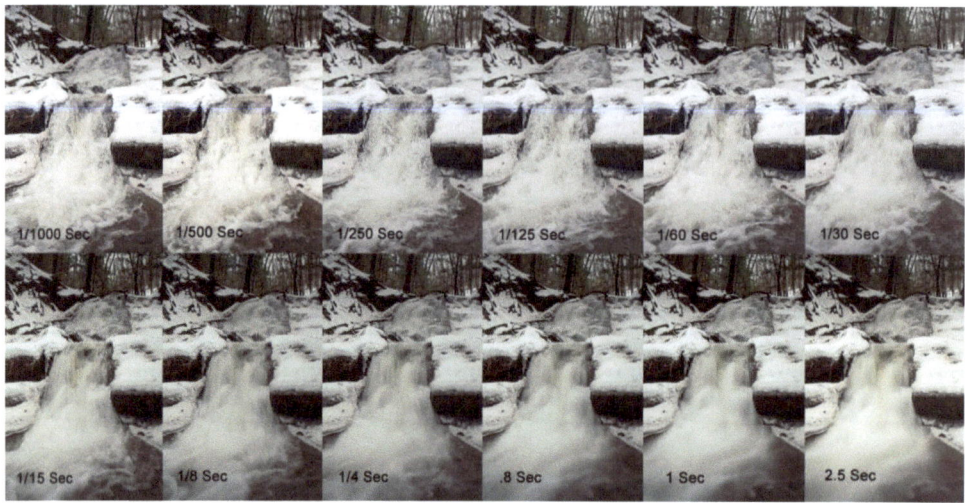

Here is a closeup of water in motion. You can really see the difference in the detail of the water as it rushes over a rock. But slow the shutter down to 1/8 second and the blur really kicks in.

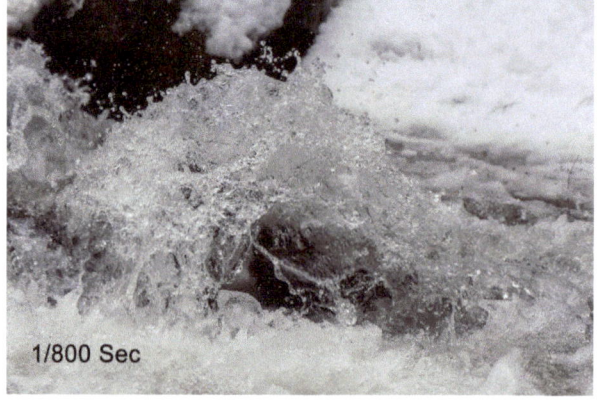

Once you get settled into a look you like, it soon becomes intuitive to pick the shutter speed that will achieve your desired results.

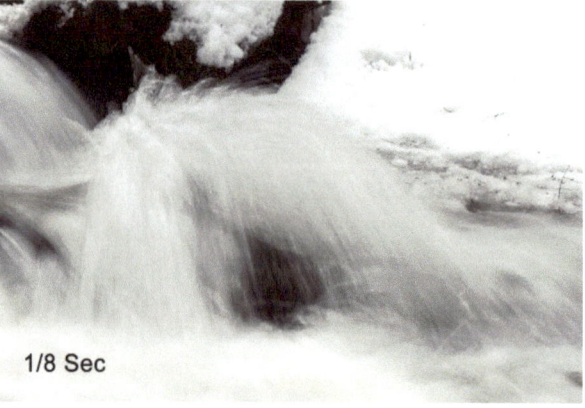

Shooting in RAW

I can't express enough the importance of capturing every image in raw format. If you have a camera that isn't capable of shooting in raw, this may be the time to upgrade. Most of the time, you'll see the letters RAW expressed in all capital letters, as if it were an acronym. It is actually not, but the argument for using all caps is so that it is distinguished as a photographic term. Whether you choose to name it raw or RAW, what this format does is preserve all of the information your camera's sensor has captured, in contrast to JPEG, which processes the image in-camera for the sake of keeping file sizes small. Once processed, the camera disposes of any information it deems irrelevant. The beauty of the raw file is that certain elements of the image such as blown out highlights or totally black shadows can be tweaked to bring out details that would otherwise have been lost in a JPEG. Other advantages to working with raw files are numerous, such as correcting white balance of entire batches of images with one click of the mouse. Think of your raw file as your digital equivalent of a film negative.

White Balance

Ever since I got serious about shooting landscapes, and waterfalls in particular, 20 years ago using film, I was constantly disappointed with color bias that poorly represented the scene as my eyes perceived it. In the days of film, we paid close attention to filtering (the physical kind that actually attached to the front of the lens!) and film types when we wanted to control color bias. Waterfall locations can absolutely wreak havoc when attempting to get accurate colors, because of the way light gets filtered through trees and bounces off of hillsides, gorges, and canyons.

In the digital world, it is easier than ever to maintain control of color balance in photos. You can use a pre-selected white balance and get close, or you can dial it in very precisely using custom white balance. Setting custom white balance is as simple as taking a photo of a white or neutral grey surface and then telling the camera to use that image when determining a baseline for white balance. If you have never attempted this, I highly recommend digging into your manual and learning! Once you've done it a few times, it becomes second nature and only takes a minute. I carry with me a collapsible white/grey disc. I mostly use the white side for setting my custom white balance, but many photographers prefer to use 18% (neutral) grey. When there is snow on the ground, I don't even use my disc; I just grab a shot of snow and set white balance according to that.

6 HIGH DYNAMIC RANGE

Perhaps the most controversial technique in the world of digital photography today is High Dynamic Range, abbreviated simply as HDR. To understand fully what the true intent of HDR is, one must look back at the "dark ages" of film. 35mm slide film, also known as transparency film, is somewhat unforgiving when it comes to dynamic range, which affects the film's exposure latitude. This range across the visible light spectrum from black to white is expressed in terms of "stops." Some of the finest photographs of the 20th Century were captured on slide film, most notably Kodak's famous Kodachrome. Slide film is only capable of capturing 5 full stops of light. In comparison, print film is capable of capturing at least 7 stops of light. However, a typical scene can have a luminance range of over 12 stops of light, which the human eye can perceive. So the traditional film landscape photographers such as Ansel Adams used techniques in their darkrooms to compensate for this shortcoming of their film, thereby producing what were technically High Dynamic Range (HDR) photos, although the term HDR never fully came into use until the 21st Century, with regard to photography. Ansel Adams and Fred Archer developed the Zone System to help themselves set the best exposures possible for large-scale scenic photos in-camera, so that less work was required in the darkroom later on.

Enter the world of the digital sensor. With all the advancements of digital photography, and there are so many I find it staggering, we are still stuck with about the same dynamic range of 5 stops on a typical digital sensor. But now, instead of a traditional darkroom, we can compensate for it via editing software. There are many ways to approach HDR photography, far too many to go into detail here. So I'll discuss the basics and you can decide how you want to go about it.

The Capture

The absolute best way to produce true HDR images is via multiple exposures over several different captures. There is software that can take a single RAW file and do a pretty good job of mimicking HDR, but it is only "pseudo" HDR, and will not hold a candle to the real deal. The most common technique used, and the one most cameras are already set up to do, is to take one normal exposure, then take one that's up to 2 stops under, then another that is up to 2 stops over. I like to go the full 2 stops in either direction, because it captures as much information as possible. I'd go further than 2 stops if my camera would let me, but currently only higher-end models can do that, at least automatically. By using AEB, or auto-exposure bracketing, one can simply start with a proper overall exposure, then set the camera to shoot -2, 0, +2 automatically with just one shutter press. Of course, this can all be done manually, but it takes a little more time, and you run the risk of bumping the camera and throwing off the alignment of the 3 images, which much be shot from the same identical place each time. If I want to go higher than +2 or lower than -2, I set my EV (exposure value) compensation above and below the high and low ends of my AEB settings to get even wider range in exposures, after I've shot a set using AEB. If you've never used EV compensation on your camera, get familiar with it, it is a valuable tool.

It is important to remember that, like shooting long exposures, shooting multiple exposures will exaggerate the blur of anything within your scene that is moving. Excessive movement will also confuse the software that attempts to render your exposures into an HDR image. It is possible to correct this "ghosting" in editing after the HDR merge; the most common and efficient method is via layer masking. Layer masking is a very valuable tool to have at your disposal for a number of reasons, so I highly recommend learning it and mastering it to expand your capabilities.

Post-Production

What you do with your multiple exposures in post-production is beyond the scope of this guide, but my workflow includes Photomatix (combines the exposures via "tonemapping"), followed by touch-up in Photoshop. The process involved in creating HDR images via software often introduces unacceptable noise, so I also recommend some sort of noise reduction software, such as Imagenomic's Noiseware Professional. Mastering the various settings and controls of the post-production software and finding a look you like is a highly personal thing that would require another entire book to cover. It takes a lot of trial-and-error and time to familiarize yourself with the tools and methods of whichever program you choose to work with.

Below is a sequence showing my three different exposures, with the fourth frame being the result of the 3 exposures combined in Photomatix. The first frame (upper left) is the camera's properly metered exposure. The frame below it is 2 stops under, and the frame in the upper right is 2 stops over.

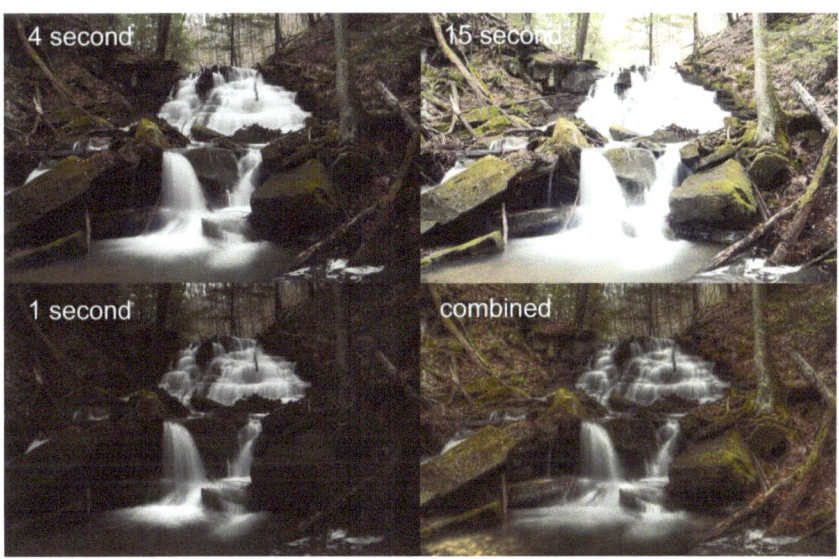

Here are larger versions of the scene captured using the camera's own best exposure setting in aperture priority mode (the 4 second exposure), and (below) the HDR processed image that combines the three total exposures.

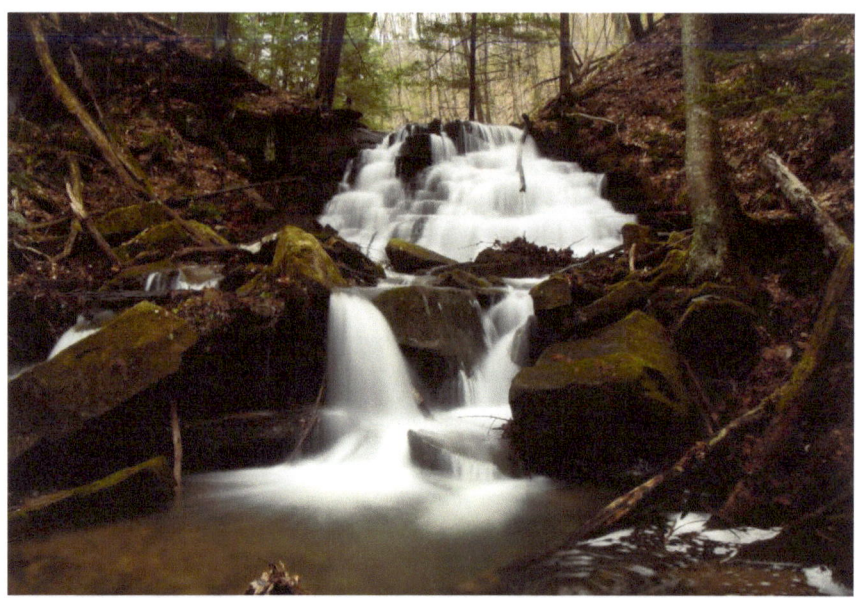

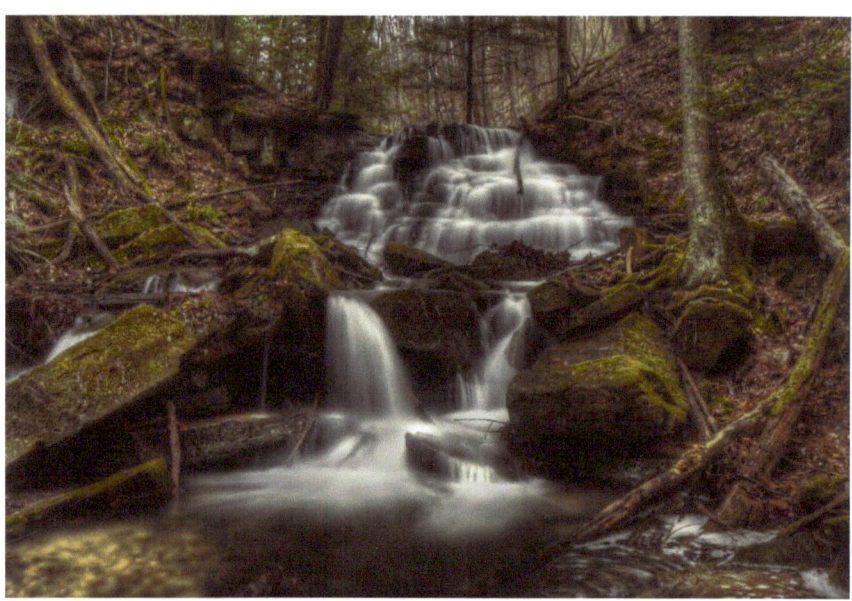

Again, I must note that there are many other ways to accomplish HDR photography, including an in-camera feature that is becoming more and more prevalent as new camera models come out. As of the date of this writing, I have yet to see any technique or feature different from the one described above that works as well. It is also possible to combine three JPEG images with proper exposure bracketing, rather than three raw file images and get excellent results; but the raw format will consistently be your best alternative.

7 PANORAMICS

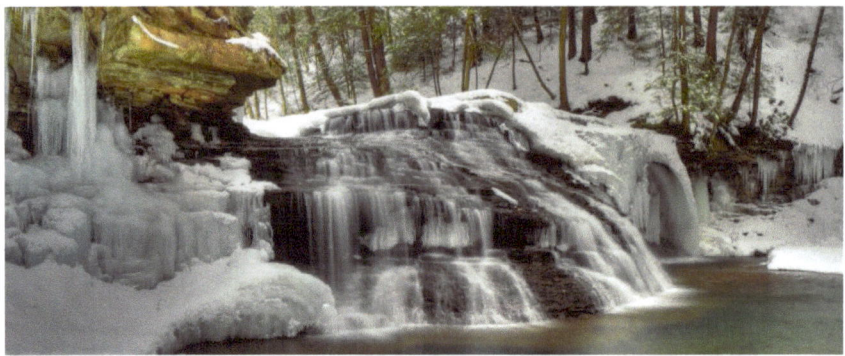

No matter how many creative angles one finds within a waterfall scene, the desire to capture the entire scene will always be there. Of course, wide-angle and ultra-wide-angle lenses can get it all in, but there will always be some level of distortion. However, a properly-done panoramic can capture a scene without any of the unnatural distortion. There are many great free stitching programs that will pull your frames together and stitch them into a panorama. I believe that the stitching feature within Photoshop is one of the best there is, so I use it. When shot properly, the only post-processing I need to do is cropping.

Here is the technique that I recommend: Shoot no wider than 35mm (on a cropped-sensor camera, such as entry-level and "pro-sumer" DSLRs) and shoot vertical. Overlap each frame by ¼ to 1/3, and make sure you give yourself enough room on the top, bottom, and ends for cropping. Tilted horizons on panoramics become very exaggerated, so take great care to keep the camera as level as possible. Rotating a stitched panoramic afterward will force you to sacrifice a lot on the top and bottom when cropping.

Here's an example of a six-frame pano prior to cropping. If you start to see a lot of arc on the upper and lower edges of the frames, you've probably shot with too wide of a focal length, and the software is going to have a hard time matching features.

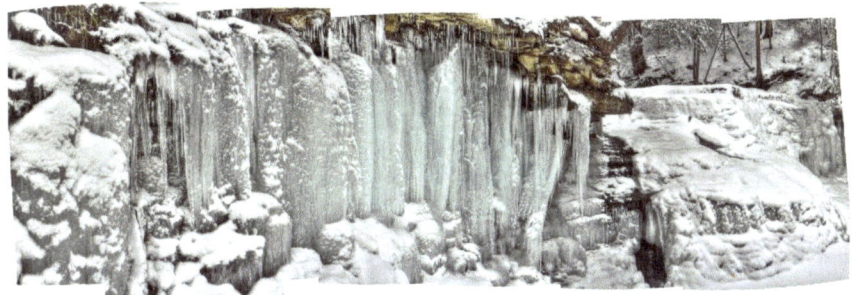

8 PREPARE FOR THE UNEXPECTED

In parting, I would like to share this story, which is a perfect example of why you should prepare for whatever may come your way as you search for the perfect waterfall photo.

A few years ago, I was camping via kayak along the Allegheny River. We set up camp near an area that I knew featured a nice little waterfall. Just as we finished setting up camp, we were approached by an Amish boy, part of a group of ten boys who had set up camp near us. They were traveling in five canoes, and had become fascinated with the waterfall while exploring the area. The boy asked me if I would take some photos of the waterfall for him, as a memento of their trip, and I could mail him the prints later.

I was happy to oblige, and then shocked when he told me eight of the ten boys wanted to be in the photo of the waterfall. So, just before dark, with my camera steadied atop my small camera bag, I shot a long exposure while the eight Amish boys stood stock-still atop the waterfall.

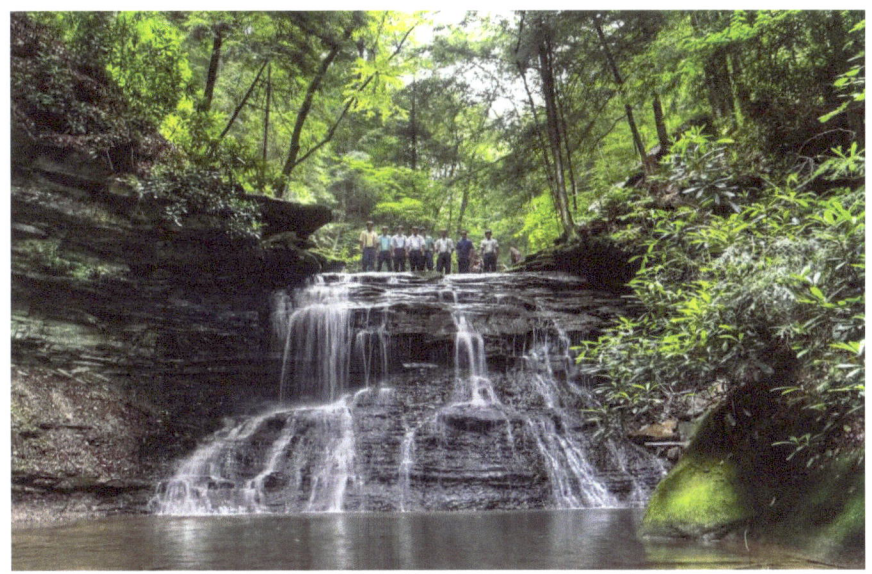

Enjoy your adventure!

ABOUT THE AUTHOR

A native and resident of northwestern Pennsylvania, Michael J. Henderson traces his roots in photography back to his early childhood. During the 1960s and '70s he logged thousands of miles with his family as they spent their vacations traveling all over the U.S., visiting beautiful locations throughout the American southwest, Pacific northwest, the Rocky Mountains, and everywhere in between. His father documented these wonderful adventures with his trusty Kodak Instamatic and Kodachrome film, and then later his stepmother introduced him to modern compact 35mm SLR cameras. It wasn't until the last few trips of that era that Mike came to realize how great it would be to carry a camera of his own; so starting out with simple, compact pocket cameras, and eventually graduating to an old second-hand Yashica 35mm SLR, he soon learned that photography could become the perfect convergence of his love for gadgetry and artistic self-expression. His very first images were actually shot with an old rollfilm twin lens reflex camera that he borrowed from his sister Linda.

By the mid-1980s, Mike began to expand on his basic knowledge of photography, delving into rules of composition and different camera techniques, including stereo (3-D) photography. By the turn of the century, Mike had already begun to embrace digital photography, and he continues to seek out new and exciting techniques to further his skills in the medium.

He is currently teaching classes at Venango College of Clarion University in Oil City, and his photos have been featured in *Pennsylvania Travel Guide, Pennsylvania Magazine, Lake Erie Lifestyle, New England Windsurfing Journal, Ultra Running, Pennsylvania Angler & Boater, and West PA Magazine,* among others.

His website is www.recordedlight.com.

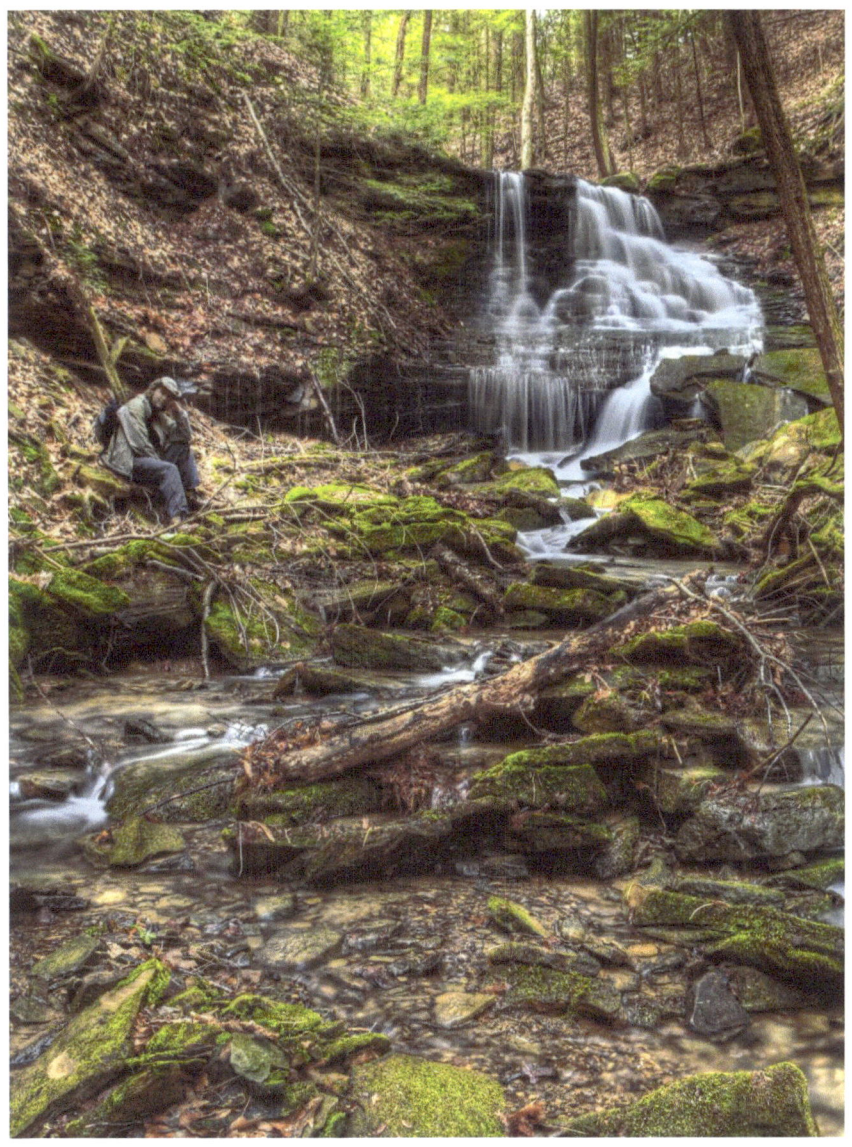

www.ingramcontent.com/pod-product-compliance
Lightning Source LLC
Chambersburg PA
CBHW040925180526
45159CB00002BA/617